PIANO · VOCAL · GUITAR

more of THE BEST ACOUSTIC ROCK SONGS EVER

ISBN 978-1-4234-3984-4

HAL•LEONARD®
CORPORATION

7777 W. BLUEMOUND RD. P.O. BOX 13819 MILWAUKEE, WI 53213

Visit Hal Leonard Online at
www.halleonard.com

ROCK SONGS EVER

AGAINST THE WIND

Words and Music by
BOB SEGER

Medium Rock beat

It seems like yes-ter-day, ___
And the years rolled slow-ly past. ___
Instrumental

but it was long a - go. ___
And I found my - self a - lone, ___

Ja - ney was love - ly. She was the queen of my nights,
sur - round - ed by stran - gers I thought were my friends.

noth - in' left ___ to burn ___ and noth - in' left to prove. ___
wor - ried a - bout pay - in', or e - ven how much I owed. ___

End instrumental

And I re - mem - ber what she ___ said to
Mov - in' eight miles a min - ute for months at a
Well, those drift - er's days are ___ past me

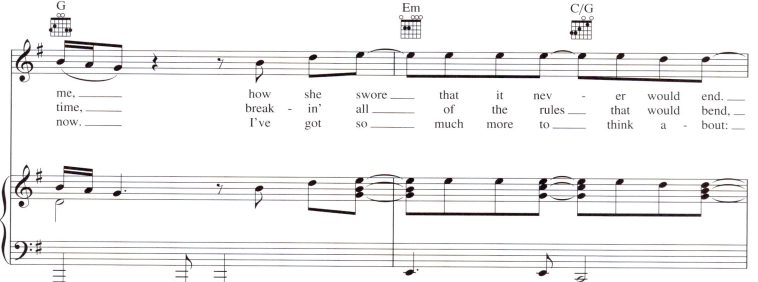

me, ___ how she swore ___ that it nev - er would end.
time, ___ break - in' all ___ of the rules ___ that would bend, ___
now. ___ I've got so ___ much more to ___ think a - bout: ___

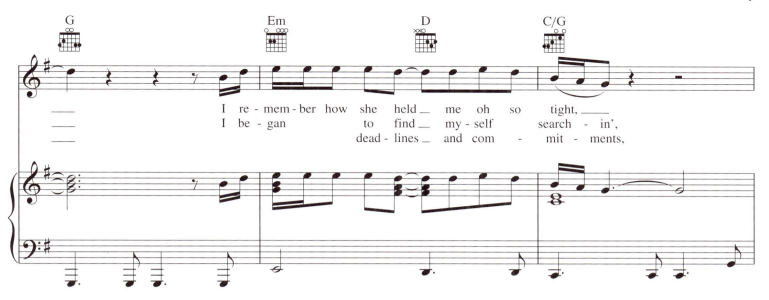

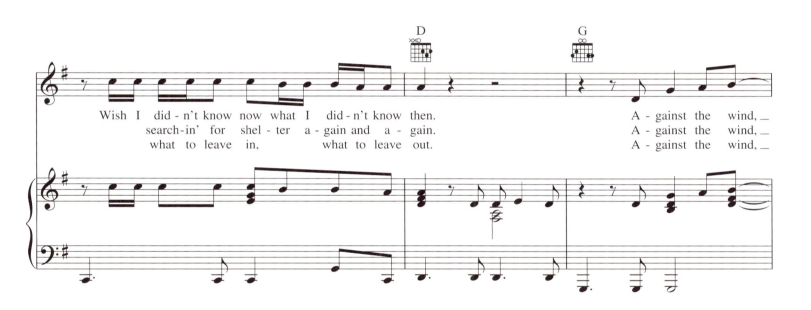

BABY, I LOVE YOUR WAY

Words and Music by
PETER FRAMPTON

Shad-ows grow __ so long __ be-fore my
Moon ap-pears __ to shine __ and light the
I can see __ the sun-set __ in your

eyes __ and they're mov-ing a-
sky with the help __ of some
eyes, brown and grey __ and

cross the page. __ Sud-den-ly __ the day __ turns in-to night __
fire-fly. __ Won-der how __ they have __ the pow'r to shine. __
blue be-sides. __ Clouds are stalk-ing is-lands in the sun. __

AMERICAN PIE

Words and Music by
DON McLEAN

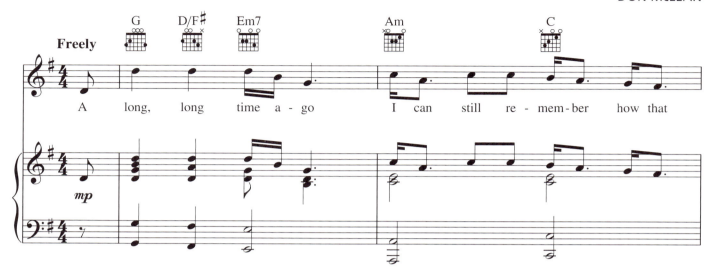

A long, long time a-go I can still re-mem-ber how that

mu-sic used to make me smile. _____ And

I knew if I had my chance that I could make those peo-ple dance and

22

day the mu - sic died. And they were sing - in'

D.S. al Coda

CODA

this - 'll be the day ___ that I ___ die. ___

Additional Lyrics

2. Now for ten years we've been on our own,
And moss grows fat on a rollin' stone
But that's not how it used to be
When the jester sang for the king and queen
In a coat he borrowed from James Dean
And a voice that came from you and me
Oh and while the king was looking down,
The jester stole his thorny crown
The courtroom was adjourned,
No verdict was returned
And while Lenin read a book on Marx
The quartet practiced in the park
And we sang dirges in the dark
The day the music died
We were singin'...bye-bye... etc.

3. Helter-skelter in the summer swelter
The birds flew off with a fallout shelter
Eight miles high and fallin' fast,
It landed foul on the grass
The players tried for a forward pass,
With the jester on the sidelines in a cast
Now the half-time air was sweet perfume
While the sergeants played a marching tune
We all got up to dance
But we never got the chance
'Cause the players tried to take the field,
The marching band refused to yield
Do you recall what was revealed
The day the music died
We started singin'... bye-bye...etc.

4. And there we were all in one place,
A generation lost in space
With no time left to start again
So come on, Jack be nimble, Jack be quick,
Jack Flash sat on a candlestick
'Cause fire is the devil's only friend
And as I watched him on the stage
My hands were clenched in fits of rage
No angel born in hell
Could break that Satan's spell
And as the flames climbed high into the night
To light the sacrificial rite
I saw Satan laughing with delight
The day the music died
He was singin'...bye-bye...etc.

AND I LOVE HER

Words and Music by JOHN LENNON
and PAUL McCARTNEY

ANNIE'S SONG

Words and Music by
JOHN DENVER

AT SEVENTEEN

Words and Music by
JANIS IAN

BABE, I'M GONNA LEAVE YOU

Words and Music by ANNE BREDON,
JIMMY PAGE and ROBERT PLANT

Additional Lyrics

I know, I know, I know, I never, I never, I never, I never, I never leave you, baby
But I got to go away from this place, I've got to quit you.
Ooh, baby, baby, baby, baby
Baby, baby, baby, ooh don't you hear it callin'?
Woman, woman, I know, I know it's good to have you back again
And I know that one day, baby, it's really gonna grow, yes it is.
We gonna go walkin' through the park every day.
Hear what I say, every day.
Baby, it's really growin', you made me happy when skies were grey.
But now I've got to go away
Baby, baby, baby, baby
That's when it's callin' me
That's when it's callin' me back home...

BAND ON THE RUN

Words and Music by PAUL
and LINDA McCARTNEY

BLAZE OF GLORY

Words and Music by
JON BON JOVI

BLACKBIRD

Words and Music by JOHN LENNON
and PAUL McCARTNEY

Slowly and smoothly

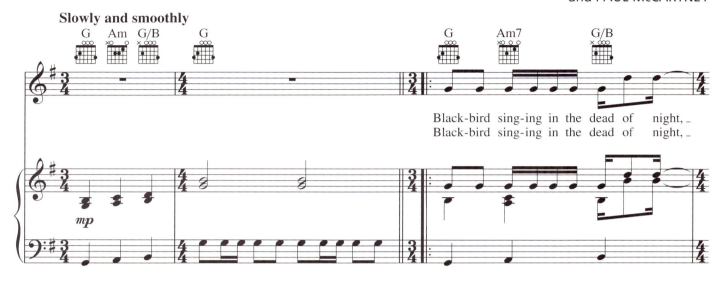

Black-bird sing-ing in the dead of night,_
Black-bird sing-ing in the dead of night,_

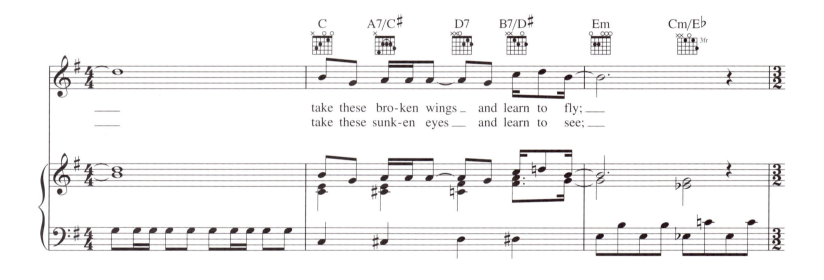

take these bro-ken wings _ and learn to fly; _
take these sunk-en eyes _ and learn to see; _

all your life _____ you were on-ly wait-ing for this mo-ment to a-
all your life _____ you were on-ly wait-ing for this mo-ment to be

BLOWIN' IN THE WIND

Words and Music by
BOB DYLAN

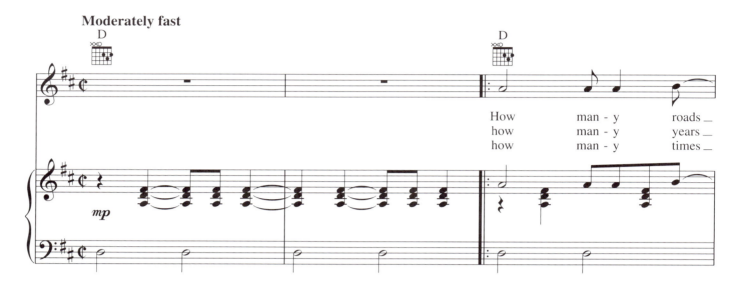

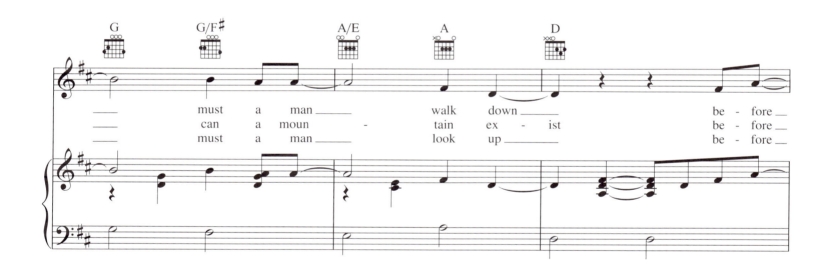

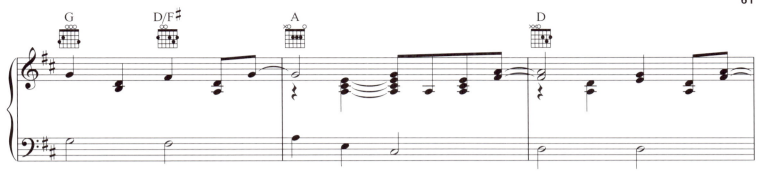

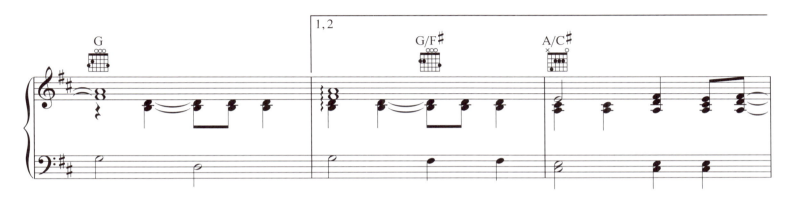

Yes, and

THE BOXER

Words and Music by
PAUL SIMON

BRIDGE OVER TROUBLED WATER

Words and Music by
PAUL SIMON

CANDLE IN THE WIND

Words and Music by ELTON JOHN
and BERNIE TAUPIN

CATCH THE WIND

Words and Music by
DONOVAN LEITCH

1. In the chil-ly hours and
(Verses 2 & 3 see additional lyrics)

mi-nutes of un-cer-tain-ty.

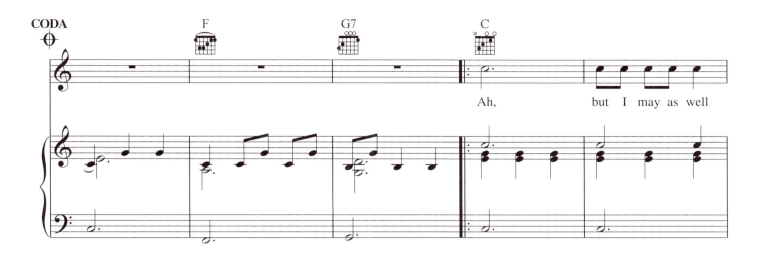

Ah, but I may as well

Repeat ad lib. and Fade

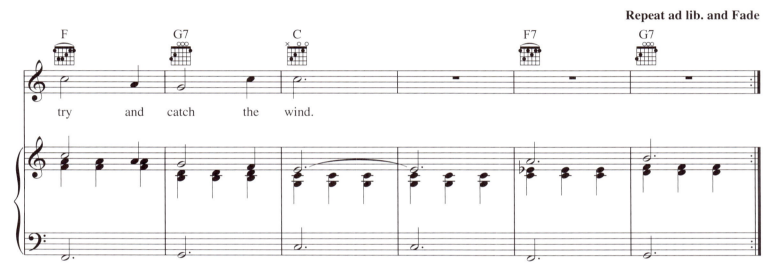

try and catch the wind.

Additional Lyrics

2. When sundown pales the sky
   I want to hide awhile
   Behind your smile
   And everywhere I'd look, your eyes I'd find.
   For me to love you now
   Would be the sweetest thing
   'Twould make me sing
   Ah but I may as well try and catch the wind.

3. When rain has hung the leaves with tears
   I want you near
   To kill my fears
   To help me leave all my blues behind
   For standing in your heart
   Is where I want to be
   And I long to be
   Ah but I may as well try and catch the wind.

CRAZY LITTLE THING CALLED LOVE

Words and Music by
FREDDIE MERCURY

mo - tor bike __ un - til I'm read - y. Cra - zy lit - tle thing called

love.

I got - ta be cool, ____ re - lax, ____

____ a - get hip, ____ a - get on my tracks. Take a

back seat, _____ hitch - hike _____ to take a lit - tle long_ ride_ on my

DANCING ON THE CEILING

Words by LIONEL RICHIE
Music by LIONEL RICHIE, CARLOS RIOS
and MICHAEL FRENCHIK

Moderate Pop

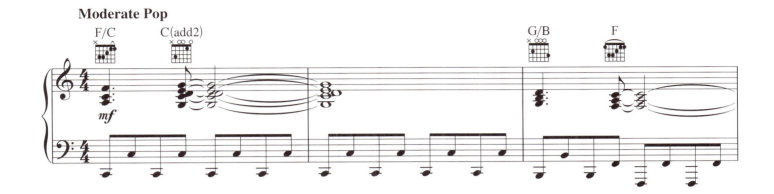

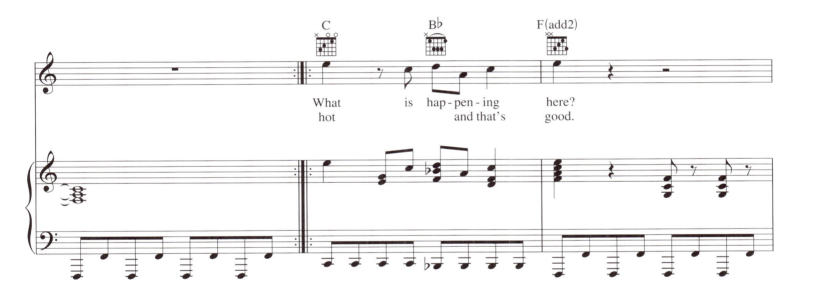

What is hap-pen-ing here?
hot and that's good.

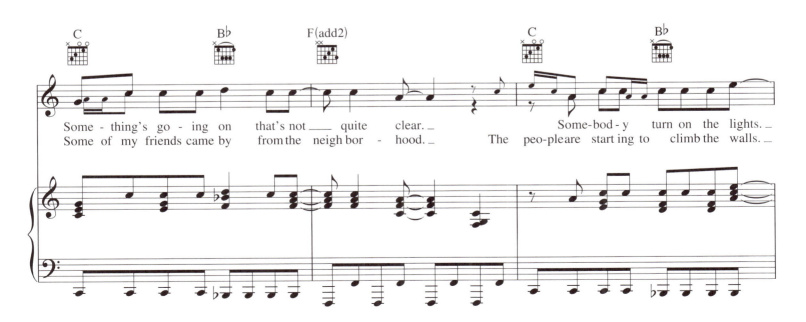

Some-thing's go-ing on that's not ___ quite clear. Some-bod-y turn on the lights. ___
Some of my friends came by from the neigh bor - hood. ___ The peo-ple are start ing to climb the walls. ___

Ev -'ry - bod - y starts to lose con - trol ___ when the mu - sic is right.

If you see ___ some - bod - y hang - in' a - round, ___ don't

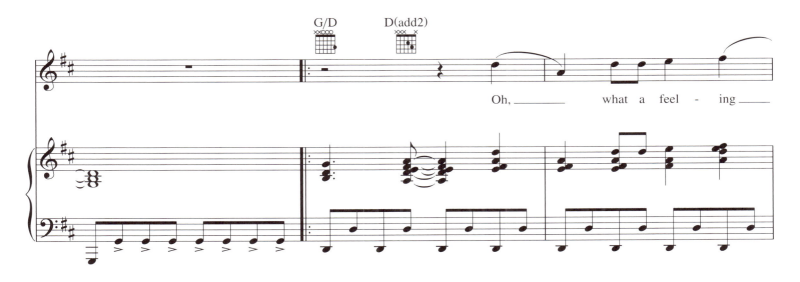

Oh, _____ what a feel - ing _____

when we're danc - ing on the ceil - ing. _____

Optional Ending

Repeat and Fade

DANIEL

Words and Music by ELTON JOHN
and BERNIE TAUPIN

Moderately fast

Dan - iel is trav -
They say Spain is pret -
Instrumental

- 'ling to - night ___ on a plane. ___
- ty, ___ 'though I've nev - er been. ___

1.
C   G7

2, 3
C

End instrumental
Oh, _____

F   C

Dan - iel, ___ my broth - er, you are old - er ___ than me. ___

F

___ Do you ___ still feel the pain ___ of the scars ___

DAYDREAM

Words and Music by
JOHN SEBASTIAN

DAUGHTER

Words and Music by STONE GROSSARD,
JEFFREY AMENT, EDDIE VEDDER, MICHAEL McCREADY
and DAVID ABBRUZZESE

Moderate Rock

A - lone, ___ list - less break-fast ta - ble in an oth-er-wise ___ emp - ty room. ___ Young ___ girl, vi - o - lins, ___ cen-ter of her own at-ten - tion. ___ But

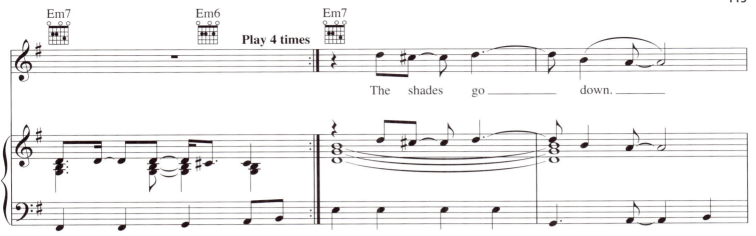

The shades go _____ down. _____

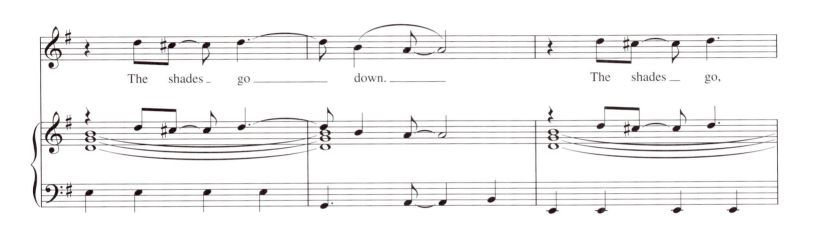

The shades _ go _____ down. _____ The shades _ go,

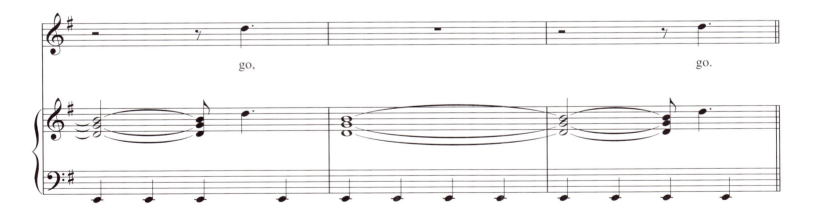

go, go.

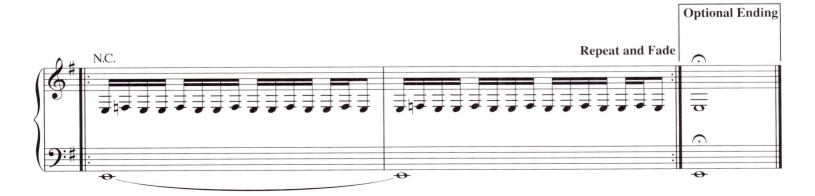

Optional Ending

Repeat and Fade

N.C.

DO YOU BELIEVE IN MAGIC

Words and Music by
JOHN SEBASTIAN

DON'T LET THE SUN GO DOWN ON ME

Words and Music by ELTON JOHN
and BERNIE TAUPIN

Slow beat

I can't ___ light no more of your dark-ness.

All my pic- tures _____ seem to fade ___ to black ___ and white. ___

THE FOOL ON THE HILL

Words and Music by JOHN LENNON
and PAUL McCARTNEY

Day af-ter day, a-lone on a hill, ___ The
Well on the way, head in a cloud, ___ The

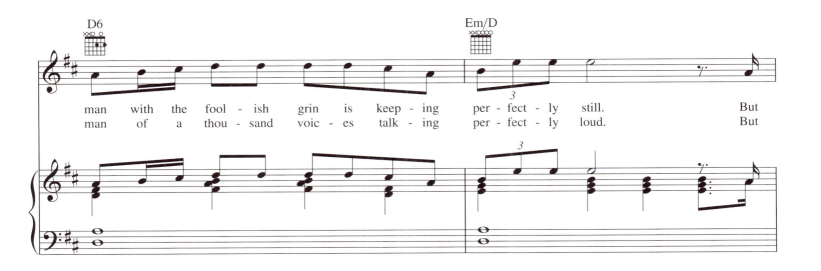

man with the fool-ish grin is keep-ing per-fect-ly still. But
man of a thou-sand voic-es talk-ing per-fect-ly loud. But

no-bod-y wants to know ___ him, They can see that he's just ___ a fool. ___ And
no-bod-y ev-er hears ___ him, Or the sound he ap-pears ___ to make. ___ And

No - bod - y seems to like _ him, They can tell what he wants _ to do, _____ And
He nev - er lis - tens to __ them, He knows that they're _ the fools, _____

he nev - er shows his feel - ings, } But the fool __ on the hill __ sees the sun _
They don't like __ him, }

__ go - ing down, _ And the eyes ___ in his head __ see the world _

__ spin - ning 'round. _

Repeat and Fade

DUST IN THE WIND

Words and Music by
KERRY LIVGREN

Moderate Folk style

Ev - 'ry - thing __ is dust in the wind.
wind.)

Repeat and Fade

Optional Ending

poco rit.

EVERY ROSE HAS ITS THORN

Words and Music by BOBBY DALL,
BRETT MICHAELS, BRUCE JOHANNESSON and RIKKI ROCKETT

Moderately

We both lie si-lent-ly still __ in the dead of the night. __ Al-though we

both lie close to-geth-er, __ we feel miles a-part __ in-side. __ Was it

some-thing I said or some-thing I did? Did my words not come out right? __ Though I

Like the knife that cuts __ you, the wound heals, but the scar, that scar re - mains.

I know I could have saved our love that night __ if I'd

known what to say. __ In - stead of mak - ing love, __ we both

made our sep - 'rate ways. __ Now I hear you've found some - bod - y new __ and

GIVE A LITTLE BIT

Words and Music by RICK DAVIES
and ROGER HODGSON

I WILL

Words and Music by JOHN LENNON
and PAUL McCARTNEY

HAVE YOU EVER SEEN THE RAIN?

Words and Music by
JOHN FOGERTY

I WRITE THE SONGS

Words and Music by
BRUCE JOHNSTON

I write the songs __ that make the
whole world sing; I write the songs _ of love and spe - cial things. _
I write the songs _ that make the young girls cry; _ I write the songs, _ I write the songs. _
Oh, my

IF

Words and Music by
DAVID GATES

Moderately, with feeling

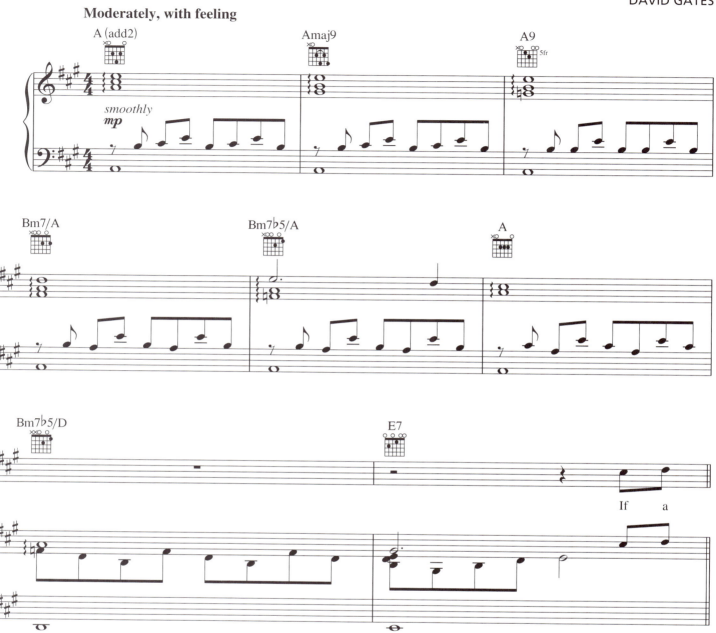

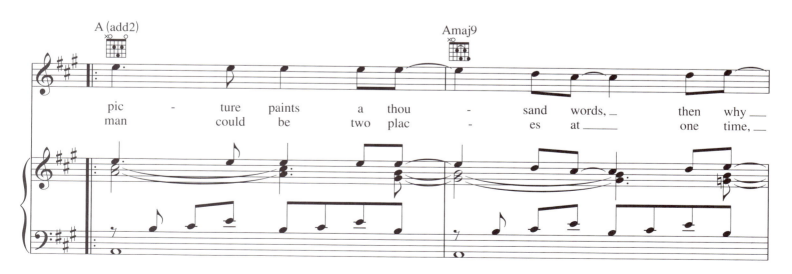

IF YOU LEAVE ME NOW

Words and Music by
PETER CETERA

-row comes, then we'll both ___ re-gret ___ the things we said ___ to - day. ___

LEARNING TO FLY

Words and Music by TOM PETTY
and JEFF LYNNE

IMAGINE

Words and Music by
JOHN LENNON

LAYLA

Words and Music by ERIC CLAPTON
and JIM GORDON

LEADER OF THE BAND

Words and Music by
DAN FOGELBERG

An on-ly child a-lone ___ and wild, ___ a cab-'net mak-er's son, ___
A qui-et man of mu - sic ___ de - nied a sim - pler fate, _

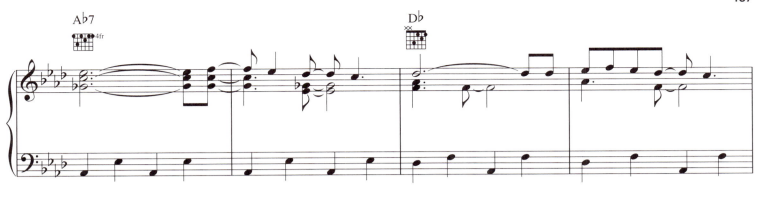

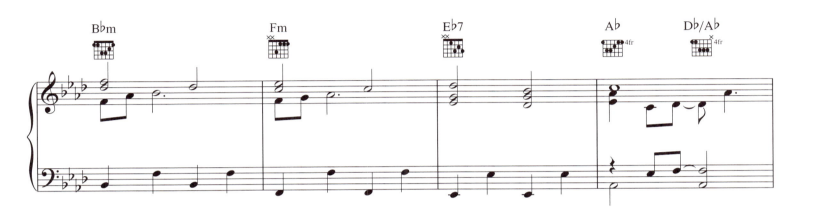

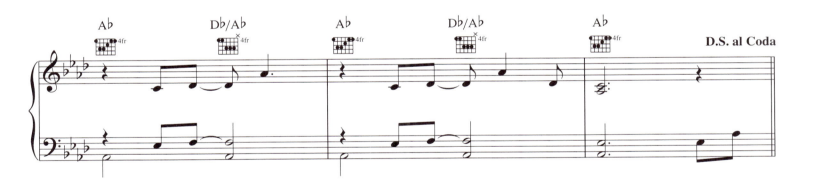

D.S. al Coda

nough.

The lead-er of the band ___ is tired ___ and ___ his

LONGER

Words and Music by
DAN FOGELBERG

LOVE SONG

Words and Music by JEFFREY KEITH
and FRANK HANNON

Keep an op - en heart and you'll find love a - gain, __ I know. you'll find love a - gain, __ I

know.

(Instrumental solo)

THE MAGIC BUS

Words and Music by
PETER TOWNSHEND

MORE THAN A FEELING

Words and Music by
TOM SCHOLZ

When I'm tired ___ and think-ing cold, I hide in my mu - sic, for -

NIGHTS IN WHITE SATIN

Words and Music by
JUSTIN HAYWARD

MY LOVE

Words and Music by
LIONEL RICHIE

Slow and steady

I've been through _ so man-y chang-es in my life, wom - an, it's a won-der I ain't lost my __ mind. _ And I ain't nev - er said how much I

NORWEGIAN WOOD
(This Bird Has Flown)

Words and Music by JOHN LENNON
and PAUL McCARTNEY

Moderately

I once had a girl, or should I say she once had me.
Instrumental

She showed me her room, is-n't it good Nor-we-gian wood. She
End instrumental She

asked me to stay and she told me to sit an-y-where, so
told me she worked in the morn-ing and start-ed to laugh, I

NOT FADE AWAY

Words and Music by CHARLES HARDIN
and NORMAN PETTY

OUR HOUSE

Words and Music by
GRAHAM NASH

Moderately slow

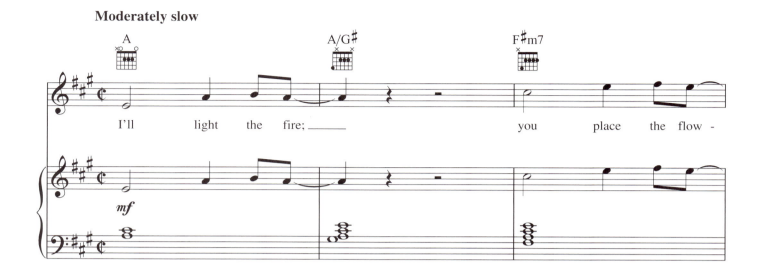

I'll light the fire; _____ you place the flow-

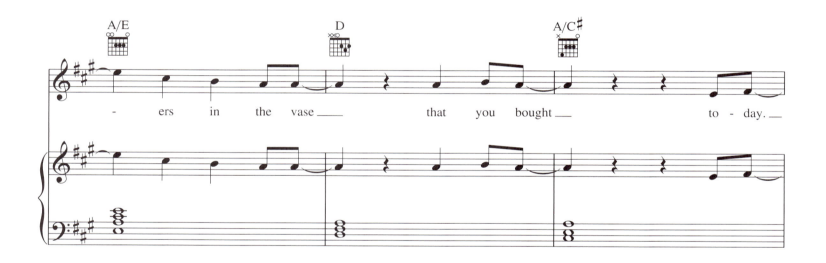

-ers in the vase _____ that you bought _____ to-day. _____

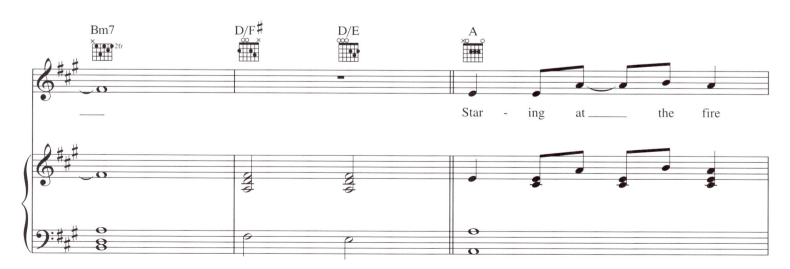

_____ Star-ing at _____ the fire

PENNY LOVER

Words and Music by LIONEL RICHIE
and BRENDA HARVEY-RICHIE

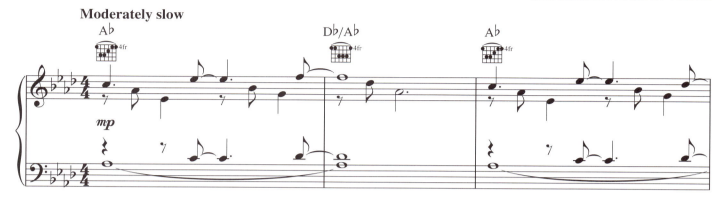

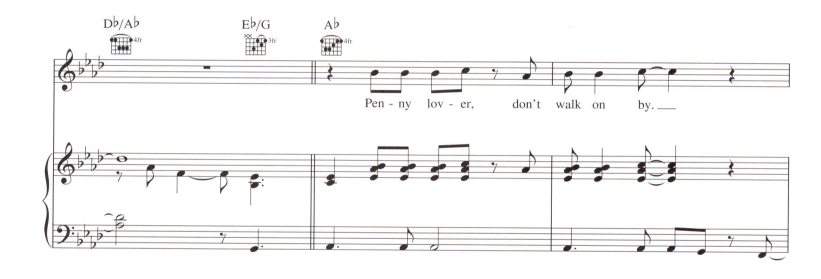

Pen-ny lov-er, don't walk on by. ___

Pen-ny lov-er, don't you make me cry. ___ Can't you see, girl, who my

PLEASE COME TO BOSTON

Words and Music by
DAVE LOGGINS

ROCKET MAN
(I Think It's Gonna Be a Long Long Time)

Words and Music by ELTON JOHN
and BERNIE TAUPIN

Moderately slow, with a beat

She packed __ my bags __ last night pre - flight, __

Ze - ro hour __ Nine A. M. __

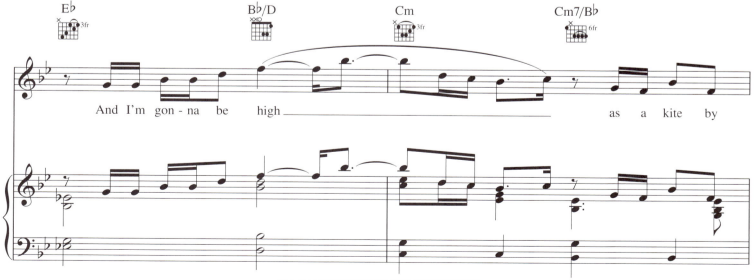

And I'm gon - na be high _____ as a kite by

them   if you did.

And all this sci-ence I don't

un-der-stand.   It's just my job five days a week.

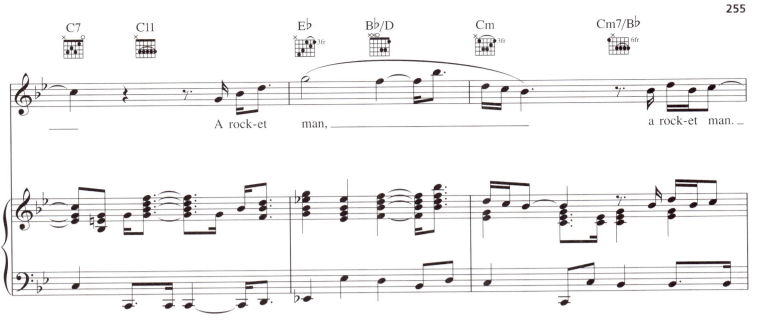

RUNNING WITH THE NIGHT

Words and Music by LIONEL RICHIE
and CYNTHIA WEIL

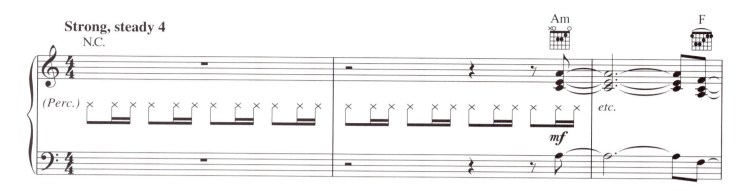

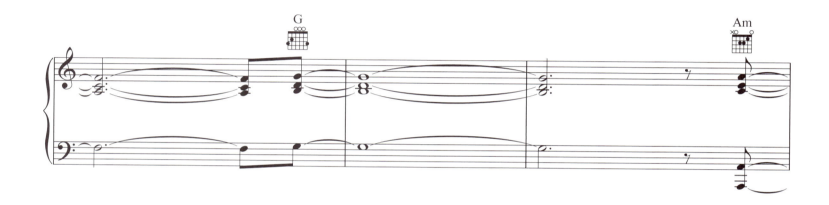

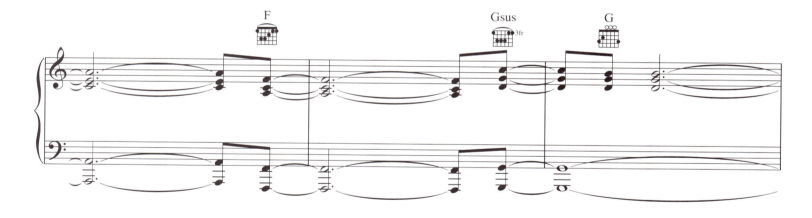

The heart of the cit - y street __ was beat - ing.

Light from the ne - ons turned the dark __

__ to day. __

We were too hot __

(Sittin' On)
THE DOCK OF THE BAY

Words and Music by STEVE CROPPER
and OTIS REDDING

SMALL TOWN

Words and Music by
JOHN MELLENCAMP

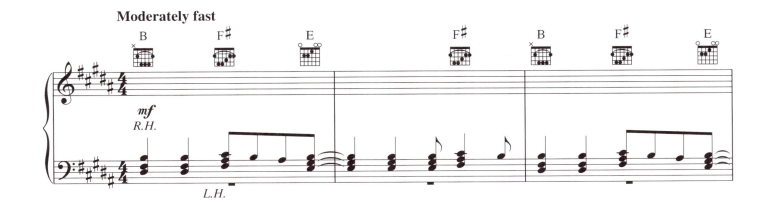

Moderately fast

Well, I was born in a small __ town,
Ed - u - cat - ed in __ a small __ town,

and I live in a small __ town;
taught the fear of Je - sus in a small town;

prob - 'ly die in a small __
used to day dream in that

SOME PEOPLE CALL IT MUSIC

Words and Music by
JOHN DAVID SOUTHER

Some peo - ple call it
The price ___ of love is

mu - sic, ___
mag - ic, ___

some peo - ple call ___ it
some - times ___ you lose ___ your

gold,
way,

no - one ___ knows. ___
but you're do - in' fine. ___

SWEET HOME CHICAGO

Words and Music by
ROBERT JOHNSON

Moderately slow Rock

*Recorded a half step lower.

SOMEONE SAVED MY LIFE TONIGHT

Words and Music by ELTON JOHN
and BERNIE TAUPIN

* *Recorded a half step higher.*

SORRY SEEMS TO BE THE HARDEST WORD

Words and Music by ELTON JOHN
and BERNIE TAUPIN

SOUTHERN CROSS

Words and Music by STEPHEN STILLS,
RICHARD CURTIS and MICHAEL CURTIS

prom - ise,   the prom - ise of a com - in' day.
come a - long make me for - get a - bout lov - ing you

So _____ I'm   in the South - ern Cross.

SUMMER BREEZE

Words and Music by JAMES SEALS
and DASH CROFTS

See the cur - tains hang - in' in the win - dow _____ in the eve - ning on a Fri - day night. _____
See the pa - per lay - in' on the side - walk, _____ a lit - tle mu - sic from the house next door. _____

A lit - tle light a shin - in' through the win - dow _____
So I walk on up to the door - step, _____

makes me feel fine, ___ blow - in' through the jas - mine in my

mind. _____

Sweet days of sum - mer the jas - mine's in bloom, __

TAKE ME HOME, COUNTRY ROADS

Words and Music by JOHN DENVER,
BILL DANOFF and TAFFY NIVERT

TEACH YOUR CHILDREN

Words and Music by
GRAHAM NASH

Teach your chil - dren
Teach your par - ents

well; their fa - ther's hell
well; their chil - dren's hell

did slow - ly go _____ by. _____ And
will slow - ly go _____ by. _____

feed then on _____ your dreams,

THIS LAND IS YOUR LAND

Words and Music by
WOODY GUTHRIE

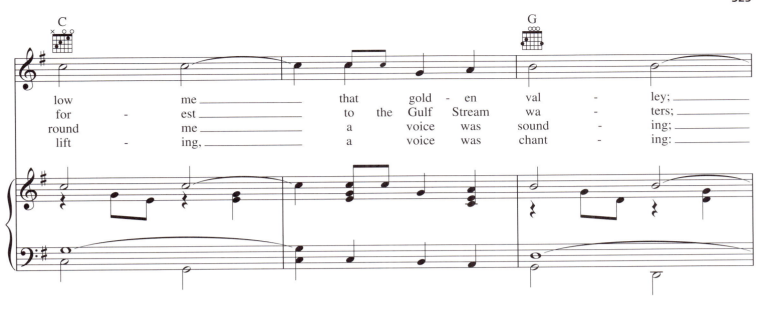

low me ____ that gold - en val - ley; ____
for - est ____ to the Gulf Stream wa - ters; ____
round me ____ a voice was sound - ing; ____
lift - ing, ____ a voice was chant - ing: ____

this land was made for you and

me. ____
2.,4.,6. This land is
3. I've roamed and me. ____
5. Well, the sun came

rit.

TIME IN A BOTTLE

Words and Music by
JIM CROCE

TO BE WITH YOU

Words and Music by ERIC MARTIN
and DAVID GRAHAME

UP ON THE ROOF

Words and Music by GERRY GOFFIN
and CAROLE KING

WAKE UP LITTLE SUSIE

Words and Music by BOUDLEAUX BRYANT
and FELICE BRYANT

Wake up, Lit-tle Su - sie, ___ wake up.

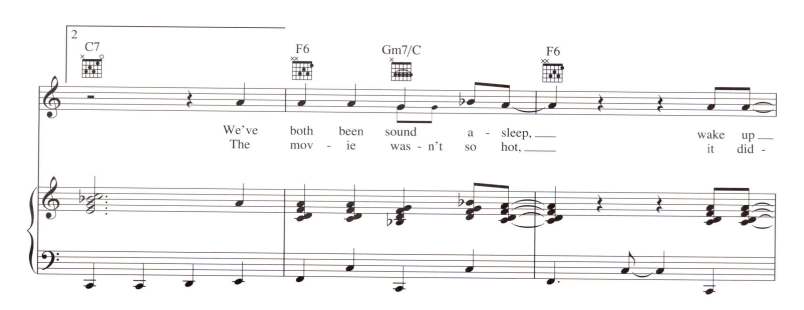

We've both been sound a - sleep, ___ wake up ___
The mov-ie was-n't so hot, ___ it did -

WANTED DEAD OR ALIVE

Words and Music by JON BON JOVI
and RICHIE SAMBORA

Moderately slow

It's

WORKING CLASS HERO

Words and Music by
JOHN LENNON

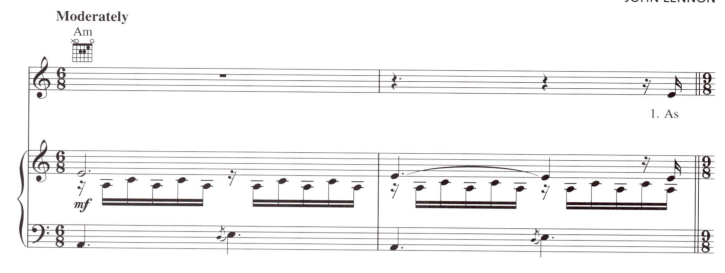

soon as you're born, _ they make you feel small _____
2. hurt you at home and they hit you at school. _____
3. tor-tured and scared you for twen-ty odd years, _____
4., 5. *(See additional lyrics)*

by giv-ing you no time in-stead of it all. _____
They hate you if you're clev-er and they de-spise a fool. _____
then they ex-pect you to pick a ca-reer. _____

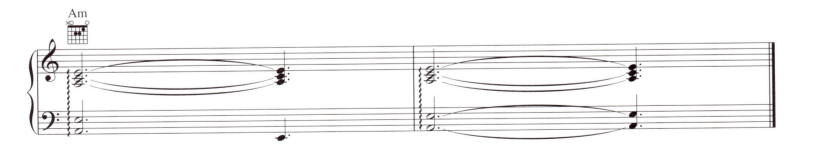

Additional Lyrics

4. Keep you doped with religion and sex and T.V.
   And you think you're so clever and classless and free.
   But you're still fucking peasants as far as I can see.
   Chorus

5. There's room at the top they are telling you still.
   But first you must learn how to smile as you kill
   If you want to be like the folks on the hill.
   Chorus

THE WORLD I KNOW

Words and Music by ED ROLAND
and ROSS BRIAN CHILDRESS

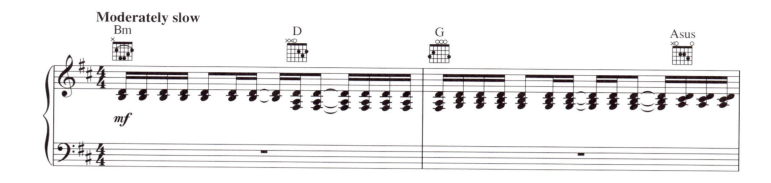

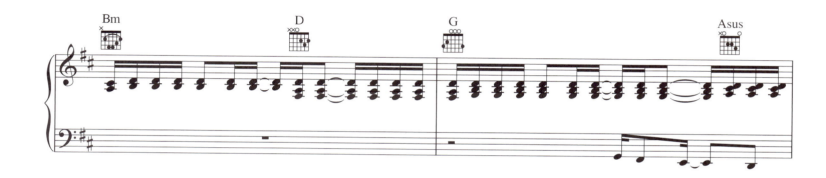

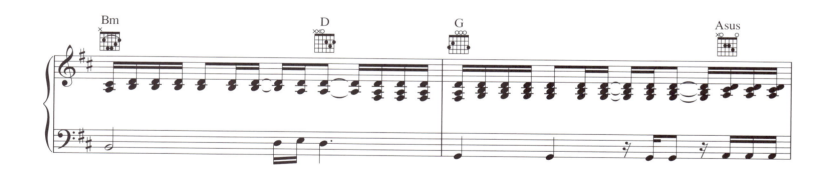

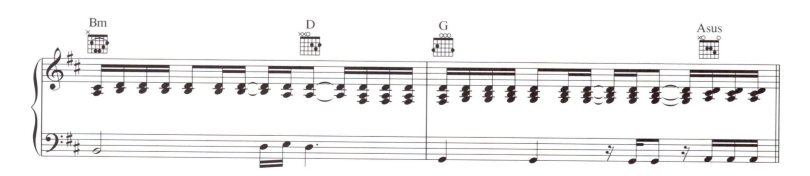

Oh, it's the world I _____ know.

You Were Meant For Me

Lyrics by JEWEL KILCHER
Music by JEWEL KILCHER and STEVE POLTZ

Easy shuffle

I hear the clock. It's six A___ M.___
I called my ma-ma, she was out for a walk.___ Con-
I brush my teeth, I put the cap back___ on.___

I feel so far from where I've___ been.___
soled a cup of cof-fee, but it did-n't want to talk.___ So, I
I know you hate it when I leave the light on.___ I

I got my eggs. I got my
picked up the pa-per, it was
pick up a cup and then I

pan - cakes, too. _____ I got my ma-ple syr - up, ev-'ry-thing but __ you. _____
more bad news. _____ My heart's be-ing bro-ken by peo-ple be-ing used. __
turn the sheets down and then I take a deep breath, a good look _ a - round. __

I break the yolks and make a smil - ey _____ face. _____ I kind - a like it in my
Put on my coat in the pour - ing _____ rain. _____ I saw a mov - ie, it just
Put on my p j's and hop in - to bed. _____ I'm half a - live, but I feel

brand new place. Wipe the spots up o - ver me, don't leave my keys in the door. _____ I
was - n't the same 'cause it was hap - py or I was sad, _____ and
most - ly dead. I try and tell my - self it'll be all right. _____

YOU'RE IN MY HEART

Words and Music by
ROD STEWART

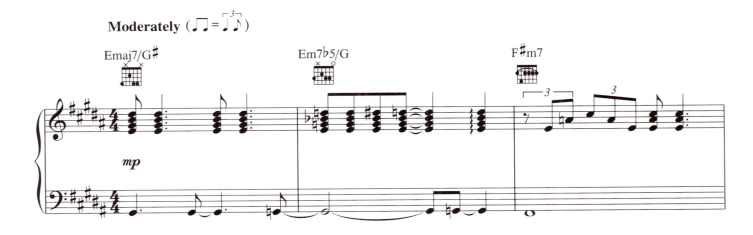

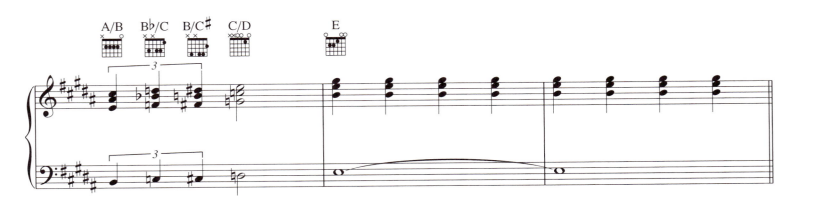

I did-n't know ___ what day it was ___ when you walked ___
I took all ___ those hab-its of yours that in the be -

YOUR SONG

Words and Music by ELTON JOHN
and BERNIE TAUPIN

Slow, but with a beat

It's a lit-tle bit fun-ny, _____ this feel-ing in-side; _____
If I was a sculp-tor, _____ but then _ a-gain, no, _____ or a

I'm not one of those _____ who _ can eas-i-ly hide. _____
man who makes po - tions in a trav-el-in' show, _____ I

Don't _ have much mon-ey, _____ but, boy, if I did, _____
know _ it's not much but it's _ the best I can do. _____

THE BEST EVER COLLECTION

ARRANGED FOR PIANO, VOICE AND GUITAR

150 of the Most Beautiful Songs Ever
150 ballads: Bewitched • (They Long to Be) Close to You • How Deep Is Your Love • I'll Be Seeing You • Unchained Melody • Yesterday • Young at Heart • more.
00360735 ....$24.95

150 More of the Most Beautiful Songs Ever
More classics include: All I Ask of You • Can You Feel the Love Tonight • Change the World • Dream a Little Dream of Me • Imagine • Let's Fall in Love • Love Me Tender • and dozens more.
00311318 P/V/G $24.95

Best Acoustic Rock Songs Ever
65 acoustic hits: Dust in the Wind • Fast Car • I Will Remember You • Landslide • Leaving on a Jet Plane • Maggie May • Tears in Heaven • Yesterday • more.
00310984 ....$19.95

Best Big Band Songs Ever
Over 60 big band hits: Boogie Woogie Bugle Boy • Don't Get Around Much Anymore • In the Mood • Moonglow • Sentimental Journey • Who's Sorry Now • more.
00359129 ....$16.95

Best Broadway Songs Ever
Over 70 songs in all! Includes: All I Ask of You • Bess, You Is My Woman • Climb Ev'ry Mountain • Comedy Tonight • If I Were a Rich Man • Ol' Man River • more!
00309155 ....$24.95

Best Children's Songs Ever
Over 100 songs: Bingo • Eensy Weensy Spider • The Farmer in the Dell • On Top of Spaghetti • Puff the Magic Dragon • Twinkle, Twinkle Little Star • and more.
00310360 (Easy Piano) $19.95

Best Christmas Songs Ever
More than 60 holiday favorites: Frosty the Snow Man • A Holly Jolly Christmas • I'll Be Home for Christmas • Rudolph, The Red-Nosed Reindeer • Silver Bells • more.
00359130 ....$19.95

Best Classic Rock Songs Ever
Over 60 hits: American Woman • Bang a Gong • Cold As Ice • Heartache Tonight • Rock and Roll All Nite • Smoke on the Water • Wonderful Tonight • and more.
00310800 ....$19.95

Best Classical Music Ever
Over 80 of classical favorites: Ave Maria • Canon in D • Eine Kleine Nachtmusik • Für Elise • Lacrymosa • Ode to Joy • William Tell Overture • and many more.
00310674 (Piano Solo) $19.95

Best Contemporary Christian Songs Ever
Over 70 favorites, including: Awesome God • El Shaddai • Friends • Jesus Freak • People Need the Lord • Place in This World • Serve the Lord • Thy Word • more.
00310558 ....$19.95

Best Country Songs Ever
78 classic country hits: Always on My Mind • Crazy • Daddy Sang Bass • Forever and Ever, Amen • God Bless the U.S.A. • I Fall to Pieces • Through the Years • more.
00359135 ....$19.95

Best Early Rock 'n' Roll Songs Ever
Over 70 songs, including: Book of Love • Crying • Do Wah Diddy Diddy • Louie, Louie • Peggy Sue • Shout • Splish Splash • Stand By Me • Tequila • and more.
00310816 ....$17.95

Best Easy Listening Songs Ever
75 mellow favorites: (They Long to Be) Close to You • Every Breath You Take • How Am I Supposed to Live Without You • Unchained Melody • more.
00359193 ....$19.95

Best Gospel Songs Ever
80 gospel songs: Amazing Grace • Daddy Sang Bass • How Great Thou Art • I'll Fly Away • Just a Closer Walk with Thee • The Old Rugged Cross • more.
00310503 ....$19.95

Best Hymns Ever
118 hymns: Abide with Me • Every Time I Feel the Spirit • He Leadeth Me • I Love to Tell the Story • Were You There? • When I Survey the Wondrous Cross • and more.
00310774 ....$18.95

Best Jazz Standards Ever
77 jazz hits: April in Paris • Beyond the Sea • Don't Get Around Much Anymore • Misty • Satin Doll • So Nice (Summer Samba) • Unforgettable • and more.
00311641 ....$19.95

More of the Best Jazz Standards Ever
74 beloved jazz hits: Ain't Misbehavin' • Blue Skies • Come Fly with Me • Honeysuckle Rose • The Lady Is a Tramp • Moon River • My Funny Valentine • and more.
00311023 ....$19.95

Best Latin Songs Ever
67 songs: Besame Mucho (Kiss Me Much) • The Girl from Ipanema • Malaguena • Slightly Out of Tune (Desafinado) • Summer Samba (So Nice) • and more.
00310355 ....$19.95

Best Love Songs Ever
65 favorite love songs, including: Endless Love • Here and Now • Love Takes Time • Misty • My Funny Valentine • So in Love • You Needed Me • Your Song.
00359198 ....$19.95

Best Movie Songs Ever
74 songs from the movies: Almost Paradise • Chariots of Fire • My Heart Will Go On • Take My Breath Away • Unchained Melody • You'll Be in My Heart • more.
00310063 ....$19.95

Best Praise & Worship Songs Ever
80 all-time favorites: Awesome God • Breathe • Here I Am to Worship • I Could Sing of Your Love Forever • Open the Eyes of My Heart • Shout to the Lord • more.
00311057 ....$19.95

Best R&B Songs Ever
66 songs, including: Baby Love • Endless Love • Here and Now • I Will Survive • Saving All My Love for You • Stand By Me • What's Going On • and more.
00310184 ....$19.95

Best Rock Songs Ever
Over 60 songs: All Shook Up • Blue Suede Shoes • Born to Be Wild • Every Breath You Take • Free Bird • Hey Jude • We Got the Beat • Wild Thing • more!
00490424 ....$18.95

Best Songs Ever
Over 70 must-own classics: Edelweiss • Love Me Tender • Memory • My Funny Valentine • Tears in Heaven • Unforgettable • A Whole New World • and more.
00359224 ....$22.95

More of the Best Songs Ever
79 more favorites: April in Paris • Candle in the Wind • Endless Love • Misty • My Blue Heaven • My Heart Will Go On • Stella by Starlight • Witchcraft • more.
00310437 ....$19.95

Best Standards Ever, Vol. 1 (A-L)
72 beautiful ballads: All the Things You Are • Bewitched • God Bless' the Child • I've Got You Under My Skin • The Lady Is a Tramp • more.
00359231 ....$17.95

Best Soul Songs Ever
70 hits include: Cry Baby • Green Onions • I Got You (I Feel Good) • In the Midnight Hour • Knock on Wood • Let's Get It On • Mustang Sally • Respect • Soul Man • What's Going On • and dozens more.
00311427 ....$19.95

More of the Best Standards Ever, Vol. 1 (A-L)
76 all-time favorites: Ain't Misbehavin' • Always • Autumn in New York • Desafinado • Fever • Fly Me to the Moon • Georgia on My Mind • and more.
00310813 ....$17.95

Best Standards Ever, Vol. 2 (M-Z)
72 songs: Makin' Whoopee • Misty • My Funny Valentine • People Will Say We're in Love • Smoke Gets in Your Eyes • Strangers in the Night • Tuxedo Junction • more.
00359232 ....$17.95

More of the Best Standards Ever, Vol. 2 (M-Z)
75 more stunning standards: Mona Lisa • Mood Indigo • Moon River • Norwegian Wood • Route 66 • Sentimental Journey • Stella by Starlight • What'll I Do? • and more.
00310814 ....$17.95

Best Torch Songs Ever
70 sad and sultry favorites: All by Myself • Crazy • Fever • I Will Remember You • Misty • Stormy Weather (Keeps Rainin' All the Time) • Unchained Melody • and more.
00311027 ....$19.95

Best TV Songs Ever
Over 50 fun and catchy theme songs: The Addams Family • The Brady Bunch • Happy Days • Mission: Impossible • Where Everybody Knows Your Name • and more!
00311048 ....$17.95

Best Wedding Songs Ever
70 songs of love and commitment: All I Ask of You • Endless Love • The Lord's Prayer • My Heart Will Go On • Trumpet Voluntary • Wedding March • and more.
00311096 ....$19.95

FOR MORE INFORMATION, SEE YOUR LOCAL MUSIC DEALER, OR WRITE TO:

HAL•LEONARD
CORPORATION
7777 W. BLUEMOUND RD. P.O. BOX 13819 MILWAUKEE, WI 53213

Visit us on-line for complete songlists at
www.halleonard.com

Prices, contents and availability subject to change without notice. Not all products available outside the U.S.A.

0308

THE ULTIMATE SONGBOOKS

HAL·LEONARD

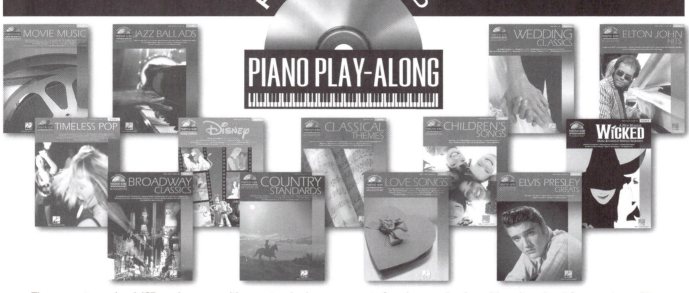

PIANO PLAY-ALONG

These great songbook/CD packs come with our standard arrangements for piano and voice with guitar chord frames plus a CD. The CD includes a full performance of each song, as well as a second track without the piano part so you can play "lead" with the band!

Vol. 1 Movie Music
00311072 P/V/G......................$14.95

Vol. 2 Jazz Ballads
00311073 P/V/G......................$14.95

Vol. 3 Timeless Pop
00311074 P/V/G......................$14.95

Vol. 4 Broadway Classics
00311075 P/V/G $14.95

Vol. 5 Disney
00311076 P/V/G......................$14.95

**Vol. 6
Country Standards**
00311077 P/V/G $14.95

Vol. 7 Love Songs
00311078 P/V/G......................$14.95

Vol. 8 Classical Themes
00311079 Piano Solo $14.95

Vol. 9 Children's Songs
0311080 P/V/G $14.95

Vol. 10 Wedding Classics
00311081 Piano Solo.................$14.95

**Vol. 11
Wedding Favorites**
00311097 P/V/G.....................$14.95

**Vol. 12
Christmas Favorites**
00311137 P/V/G $14.95

**Vol. 13
Yuletide Favorites**
00311138 P/V/G.....................$14.95

Vol. 14 Pop Ballads
00311145 P/V/G......................$14.95

**Vol. 15
Favorite Standards**
00311146 P/V/G......................$14.95

Vol. 16 TV Classics
00311147 P/V/G......................$14.95

Vol. 17 Movie Favorites
00311148 P/V/G......................$14.95

Vol. 18 Jazz Standards
00311149 P/V/G......................$14.95

**Vol. 19
Contemporary Hits**
00311162 P/V/G......................$14.95

Vol. 20 R&B Ballads
00311163 P/V/G......................$14.95

Vol. 21 Big Band
00311164 P/V/G......................$14.95

Vol. 22 Rock Classics
00311165 P/V/G......................$14.95

Vol. 23 Worship Classics
00311166 P/V/G......................$14.95

Vol. 24 Les Misérables
00311169 P/V/G......................$14.95

**Vol. 25
The Sound of Music**
00311175 P/V/G......................$14.95

**Vol. 26 Andrew Lloyd
Webber Favorites**
00311178 P/V/G......................$14.95

**Vol. 27 Andrew Lloyd
Webber Greats**
00311179 P/V/G......................$14.95

**Vol. 28
Lennon & McCartney**
00311180 P/V/G......................$14.95

Vol. 29 The Beach Boys
00311181 P/V/G......................$14.95

Vol. 30 Elton John
00311182 P/V/G......................$14.95

Vol. 31 Carpenters
00311183 P/V/G......................$14.95

**Vol. 32
Bacharach & David**
00311218 P/V/G......................$14.95

Vol. 33 Peanuts™
00311227 P/V/G......................$14.95

**Vol. 34 Charlie Brown
Christmas**
00311228 P/V/G......................$14.95

**Vol. 35
Elvis Presley Hits**
00311230 P/V/G......................$14.95

**Vol. 36
Elvis Presley Greats**
00311231 P/V/G......................$14.95

**Vol. 37 Contemporary
Christian**
00311232 P/V/G......................$14.95

**Vol. 38 Duke Ellington –
Standards**
00311233 P/V/G......................$14.95

**Vol. 39 Duke Ellington –
Classics**
00311234 P/V/G......................$14.95

Vol. 40 Showtunes
00311237 P/V/G......................$14.95

**Vol. 41
Rodgers & Hammerstein**
00311238 P/V/G......................$14.95

Vol. 42 Irving Berlin
00311339 P/V/G......................$14.95

Vol. 43 Jerome Kern
00311340 P/V/G......................$14.95

**Vol. 44 Frank Sinatra –
Popular Hits**
00311377 P/V/G......................$14.95

**Vol. 45 Frank Sinatra –
Most Requested Songs**
00311378 P/V/G......................$14.95

Vol. 46 Wicked
00311317 P/V/G......................$14.95

Vol. 47 Rent
00311319 P/V/G......................$14.95

**Vol. 48
Christmas Carols**
00311332 P/V/G......................$14.95

Vol. 49 Holiday Hits
00311333 P/V/G......................$14.95

**Vol. 51
High School Musical**
00311421 P/V/G......................$19.95

**Vol. 52 Andrew Lloyd
Webber Classics**
00311422 P/V/G......................$14.95

Vol. 53 Grease
00311450 P/V/G......................$14.95

**Vol. 54
Broadway Favorites**
00311451 P/V/G......................$14.95

Vol. 55 The 1940s
00311453 P/V/G......................$14.95

Vol. 56 The 1950s
00311459 P/V/G......................$14.95

**Vol. 63
High School Musical 2**
00311470 P/V/G......................$19.95

**Vol. 64
God Bless America**
00311489 P/V/G......................$14.95

Vol. 65 Casting Crowns
00311494 P/V/G......................$14.95

FOR MORE INFORMATION, SEE YOUR LOCAL MUSIC DEALER,
OR WRITE TO:

HAL·LEONARD®
CORPORATION

7777 W. BLUEMOUND RD. P.O. BOX 13819 MILWAUKEE, WI 53213
Visit Hal Leonard Online at www.halleonard.com

Prices, contents, and availability subject to change without notice.
Disney characters and artwork © Disney Enterprises, Inc.

0108